MAKING DISCIPLES

FOLLOWING JESUS' MODEL

Mike Flynn

Fresh Wind
MINISTRIES

FreshWind Ministries

4406 El Corazon Ct.
Camarillo, CA 93012

Printed in the United States of America.

All Scripture quotations, unless otherwise indicated, are from
the THE HOLY BIBLE, NEW INTERNATIONAL VERSION.
Copyright © 1973, 1978, 1984 by International Bible Society.
Used by permission of Zondervan Publishing House.
All rights reserved.

Cover and book design by Mike Rutland/MDR Design.

FIRST EDITION   REPRINTED 2007

ISBN: 0-9656897-1-9

07 08 09   10 9 8 7 6 5 4 3 2

This edition is printed on acid-free paper that meets the
American National Standards Institute Z.39.48 Standard.

In memory of
Sam Agajanian
A great disciple
and discipler

TABLE OF CONTENTS

Introduction

> *"Go and
> make disciples."*
> Matthew 28:19

This is not a sophisticated book. It describes several elements by which Jesus modeled the making of disciples. I am using the term "discipling" to express the investing of one's life into another. There are very worthwhile and sophisticated shadings of this investment—mentor, coach, spiritual guide, counselor, teacher, sponsor, model—and I have profited from those distinctions. But I wish to maintain that when Jesus gave the command, "make disciples," He did not impose an impossible or overly complicated task upon the everyday, normal believer, but one which is quite achievable. So I am simply using the word "discipling" to sum up all the shadings indicated by other terms.

A season has begun in which sophisticated shadings of meaning will be less appropriate than they are today. We are going to need people who have a simplified view of what needs to take place.

THE HARVEST

We are in the springtime of a harvest. The signs are everywhere. In the natural world signs of harvest first appear as tender sprouts and warmer days and the putting forth of new growth. So also in the spiritual world there are signs that a great harvest is beginning.

For example, there is a world-wide refreshing of the people of God; there is an enormous enlargement of understanding of the power and practices of prayer; social-spiritual dynamics are also there for the observing—the Promise Keepers movement, for example—; new missions agencies are springing up almost every day, and older agencies are finding themselves renewed and reinvigorated; the number of unreached people-groups is declining rapidly.

For those with the worldview lenses to see them, there are miracles popping up everywhere, especially in the more spiritually-attuned third world. It is almost commonplace to hear of miracles, healings, even raisings from the dead in many parts of the world.

The Word of God is going forth with power and with a vigor that could only have been dreamed about a quarter century ago. There is a veritable explosion of the Word's proclamation and availability in the third world.

Even the media—long hostile to even the most unthreatening religious values—is increasingly producing fair and balanced articles about spiritual truths and dynamics. It is becoming more acceptable for celebrities to proclaim their faith without being ridiculed.

These few signs which I have mentioned could be elaborated greatly. I simply note them briefly to indicate that there is much evidence of an outpouring of God's grace to harvest men, women, and children into his kingdom.

But the question I want to focus on is "what will we do with the new converts?" More to the point perhaps, "what should we do with the converts we already have?" While the Spirit of God convicts and enables people to say "Jesus is Lord," He relies on human beings to participate in that convicting and then enabling and molding his people into followers of Jesus Christ. God is an incarnationalist up to his hairline: He is committed to working with and through and among and for people. So, what are we going to do with them?

DISCIPLE-MAKING

In the space of three years, Jesus of Nazareth fed thousands, healed hundreds, and trained twelve. It wasn't the thousands He fed who spread Christianity through the known world. Nor was it the hundreds He healed. Rather, it was the twelve He trained, and those they trained, who took the message of the Good News to the nations. This, of course, is not to downplay getting fed and healed; it is rather to play up the importance of getting trained and training others.

The briefest version of the Great Commission is contained in those two words: *make disciples*. It does not stop with making believers or churchmen—which are easier to produce than disciples. You can produce believers and churchmen without producing disciples.

WHAT IS A DISCIPLE?

A disciple is a converted and baptized person who has been taught to "obey everything I have commanded you" (Matthew 28:20). Teaching and obedience are keys to being discipled. You see right away that it takes two parties to produce a disciple: one who teaches and one who obeys. The discipler teaches; the disciple obeys.

Some years ago it occurred to me to try to weigh Jesus' commands in order to determine some sense of priority of what to obey. I found out that the first four of his commands were these: 1st, love; 2nd, believe; 3rd, watch; 4th, forgive. Trying to obey those four commands has kept me pretty busy. Along the way I have learned a fair bit about what each of them means. To the degree that I live in obedience to those commands, I have become his disciple. To the degree that I teach others what those commands mean and to the degree that they obey, they have become his disciples.

Jesus, of course, is the real discipler. We are simply his flesh and blood helpers. We want to lead people into obedience to him, not to us. But there also needs to be a responsiveness to us for it all to work.

"Teaching" and "obedience" are compacted words, requiring considerable unpacking and decompacting. As I have worked to be discipled and make disciples, I have observed that Jesus practiced seven behaviors as He made his disciples. These seven behaviors sufficiently unpack "teaching" and "obedience" so that we can follow through successfully on his command to produce disciples. He who said "follow me" modeled for us what it is to make disciples. My experience is that if we try to imitate these behaviors in the power and wisdom Jesus gives, we will find that we too have produced disciples for Jesus Christ. Each of chapters one through seven deals with one of these behaviors.

No one person will find him or herself equally skilled at each of Jesus' behaviors. But each will find one or two at which he can excel, trusting the Lord to provide other behaviors through other disciplers. As we zip through this little book, I invite you to assess which of these behaviors have been done for you and which you seem to be inclined to do for others.

As I describe the behaviors that Jesus used to make disciples, I will also suggest the *focus* of these behaviors in order to pinpoint the goals Jesus was meeting. As well as asking which behaviors have been done for you, you might consider which of these focuses have been made real in your life, which have been accomplished, and which are yet to be achieved.

Finally, do not hastily disqualify yourself from the making of disciples. I say this because I regularly run into people who shrink back from even considering that they could make disciples for Jesus. Jesus directed the Great Commission to *anyone* who took it seriously. A discipler does not have to possess great skill, education, IQ, ordination papers, commendation, or experience to make disciples. A heart for them will do quite nicely. Remember what St. Paul said to the Corinthians: "Brothers, think of what you were when you were called. Not many of you were wise by human standards; not many were influential; not many were of noble birth" (I Corinthians 1:26). If you do one or more of Jesus' behaviors for them, you'll have contributed mightily towards the advancement of the kingdom of God.

YOU, THE DISCIPLE

At the Last Supper, Jesus noticed that the disciples were still jockeying for position, arguing who among them would be the greatest. He decided to end this incessant proud competition by assuming the role of a slave *Himself.* So He began washing their feet. When He came to Peter, Peter refused to have his feet washed. Now that Jesus was the one performing that menial task, Peter was ashamed to let him do it for him. "You shall never wash my feet," Peter exclaimed. Note what Jesus replied, "Unless I wash you, you have no part with me." (John 13:8)

Why did Jesus say that? He seemed ready to discard three years of investment in Peter and disqualify him from being a disciple over this one issue of washing his feet. The answer is simply this: *you can't give away what you don't have.* The prime qualification for ministering to others is having received ministry oneself. Those who have been taught make good teachers, those who have been healed make good healers, those who have been evangelized make good evangelists, those who have been well forgiven make good forgivers.

While most of this book deals with the skills of being discipled and making disciples of others, it is crucial not to miss the matter of character. Peter's character was out of whack in the matter of pride. He was both too proud to volunteer to wash others' feet and too proud to accept Jesus' washing of his feet. Jesus regarded it as being so important that it was a do or die. "Either you deal with your pride and let Me wash your feet or we're through," was the message.

How would Peter ever successfully navigate through the pride issues of others if he hadn't dealt with them himself? How could he be used by God to bring others to humility if he hadn't been brought there himself? You see, you've got to be a disciple before you can be a discipler. That doesn't mean that you have to put discipling of others on hold for the next 25 years until you get all your issues dealt with, but it does mean that you've put yourself in the place of being a receiver before you presume to be a giver.

To that end, let's look at one biblical example of a fine receiver, Elisha. Elisha's discipler was Elijah. Elijah had been told to conscript Elisha into service at God's direction while he was on retreat on Mt. Horeb, "and anoint Elisha son of Shaphat from Abel Meholah to succeed you as prophet." (1 Kings 19:16) Elijah's response was to find Elisha and throw his cloak around him. The cloak was the symbol of his office as prophet. Elisha knew instantly what that action meant and begged "'Let me kiss my father and mother good-by and then I will come with you.' 'Go back,' Elijah replied, 'What have I done to you?'"

Elisha was saying, "let me wrap things up here and then I'll go with you," but Elijah was put off by this delay. So Elisha met this rebuke with a sell-all-burn-the-bridges response. He slaughtered his oxen and barbecued them using the plow as fuel. That is, he liquidated everything with which he made a living as a farmer. "Then he set out to follow Elijah and became his attendant." (verse 21)

For the next ten years Elisha followed Elijah around, serving him, watching how he worked, learning the trade of being a prophet. These ten years required the humility to be a learner, to be a follower, to be a receiver. Elisha learned well. When it came time for Elijah to leave this earth, we see Elisha exemplifying one last quality in being a disciple.

The story takes up in 2 Kings 2. "When the Lord was about to take Elijah up to heaven in a whirlwind, Elijah and Elisha were on their way from Gilgal. Elijah said to Elisha, 'Stay here; the Lord has sent me to Bethel.' But Elisha said, 'As surely as the Lord lives and as you live, I will not leave you.' So they went down to Bethel." (verses 1-2) What was happening here was a test. You see, Elisha wanted the anointing that Elijah had, but here was his own master suggesting another course to take. But Elisha passed the test by refusing to be shaken loose from Elijah.

At Bethel, the test grew. The prophets taunted Elisha, "Do you know that the Lord is going to take your master from you today?" Yes, he replied, but shut up about it. The test grew yet larger when Elijah told Elisha to stay there with those very prophets who had taunted him. Again he refused to let Elijah get away from him.

The same test was repeated at Jericho. In other words, Elijah tried *three times* to shake off Elisha but Elisha refused to be put aside. It was as though Elisha said, "Why should I go to seminary when you are the one who has the anointing that I want. You're not getting out of my sight!"

So they arrive at the Jordan. Elijah takes the symbol of his office as a prophet, that cloak he had thrown over Elisha's shoulders 10 years before, rolls it up and strikes the surface of the Jordan with it. Immediately the waters part and the two of them walk over on dry land. "When they had crossed, Elijah said to Elisha, 'Tell me, what can I do for you before I am taken from you?'" It's as though he said, "OK, Kid, you've passed the test. What do you want for your reward?"

"Let me inherit a double portion of your spirit," Elisha replied. I think this request pleased Elijah no end. His disciple wanted twice the anointing that was on him! But he determined to let God decide if the wish would be granted, "if you see me when I am taken from you, it will be yours—otherwise not."

"As they were walking along and talking together, suddenly a chariot of fire and horses of fire appeared and separated the two of them, and Elijah went up to heaven in a whirlwind. Elisha saw this and cried out, 'My father! My father! The chariots and horsemen of Israel!'" Elisha saw the whole thing and proved it by shouting out what he saw.

Note what he did next. "Then he took hold

of his own clothes and tore them apart." It was as though he was saying, "I've had it with *my* anointing. I'm done with it now."

"He picked up the cloak that had fallen from Elijah and went back and stood on the bank of the Jordan. Then he took the cloak and struck the water with it. 'Where is now the Lord, the God of Elijah?' he asked. The water divided to the right and to the left, and he crossed over." This was the proof that Elijah's anointing had fallen on him. Was it a double anointing? Only time would tell.

What can we learn from the example of Elisha?

First, when it seems as though God has gifted someone else with something you want, stay with that person as much as you can watching them operate, learning from them, catching the drift of their ministry.

Second, don't let other plausible options shake you loose from getting all that you want from that person or those persons. If necessary, be a pest until you get what you need.

Third, realize that while some of the giftings you possess are there simply by virtue of creation, education, salvation, and in-filling, yet the fullness of these and other giftings takes the investment of someone else in you. Anointings are transferable: stick close to those who have what you want until they are transferred to you.

Finally, once you have some sense that your discipler's anointing now rests on you, go out and use it as soon as possible.

In the next seven chapters, as we look at Jesus' behaviors towards the twelve disciples, keep asking yourself, "Has this been done for me? By whom? If not, does God want me to profit from this behavior? If so, who could I go to in order to receive it?"

Remember, you can only give to others what's been given to you.

Before we end this introduction, let's look at some ways to enter into a discipling relationship. It's easy, of course, if someone comes to you and invites you to tag along with them. By the time you finish this book, I hope you begin to see that you might perform that service for others. At the moment, few in the Body of Christ seem to have a vision for that kind of relationship. That's something I hope this book will be used to correct.

But you don't have to wait until someone gets a message on a holy mountain to throw their cloak around your shoulders. You can approach them. This can be pretty simple and straightforward. You just walk up to someone whose ministry you've observed at work and say, "I notice that you seem gifted in the ministry of _____ (helping, organizing, teaching, healing, leading, worship leading, prophecy, witnessing, relating, resolving conflict, training, counseling, leading small groups, leading Bible studies, etc.) I would like to learn that ministry. Do you mind if I try to learn from you?"

Another thing to think of and negotiate is how long your relationship might last. "How about once a week for three months? Then maybe we'll re-up." Discuss the skills you'd like to learn in as great detail as possible. Just hearing your friend talk about his or her ministry will start the process of learning. What might your role be?

At first, you might be comfortable only in observing. Later you might help your guide in some fashion. Later yet you could try your hand at doing some part of the ministry with the safety net of his or her presence to catch you if you need it. The remaining chapters will give much clarity concerning what to expect and talk over.

1

He Prayed For them

"I pray for them."
John 17:8

BEHAVIOR: HE PRAYED FOR THEM
FOCUS: SELECTION, PROTECTION, UNITY

SELECTION. Luke tells us that Jesus spent a whole night in prayer before choosing the twelve (6:12-13). I have often joked that it took all night because He selected candidates you and I would not choose, requiring Him to take time to hear the Father single out each of them. One of my favorite pieces of literature is the following letter which hopped from one church bulletin to another a few years ago:

July 1, AD 30
Jesus, Son of Joseph
Woodcrafters Carpenter Shop
Nazareth 25922

Dear Sir:

Thank you for submitting the résumés of the twelve men you have picked for management positions in your new organization. All of them have now taken our battery of tests; and we have not only run the results through our computer, but also arranged personal interviews for each of them with our psychologist and vocational aptitude consultant.

The profiles of all tests are included, and you will want to study each of them carefully.

As part of our service and for your guidance, we make some general comments, much as an auditor will include general statements. This is given as a result of staff consultation and come without any additional fee.

It is the staff opinion that most of your nominees are lacking in background, education and vocational aptitude for the type of enterprise you are undertaking. They do not have the team concept. We would recommend that you continue your search for persons of experience in managerial ability and proven capability.

Simon Peter is emotionally unstable and given to fits of temper. Andrew has absolutely no qualities of leadership. The two brothers, James and John, the sons of Zebedee, place personal interest above company loyalty. Thomas demonstrates a questioning attitude that would tend to undermine morale. We feel that it is our duty to tell you that Matthew has been blacklisted by the Greater Jerusalem Better Business Bureau. James, the son of Alphaeus, and Thaddeus definitely have radical leanings, and they both registered a high score on the manic-depressive scale.

One of the candidates, however, shows great potential. He is a man of ability and resourcefulness, meets people well, has a keen business mind and has contact in high places. He is highly motivated, ambitious and responsible. We recommend Judas Iscariot as your controller and right-hand man. All of the other profiles are self explanatory.

We wish you every success in your new venture.

Sincerely yours,

Jordan Management Consultants

We're so used to lauding the disciples that this letter may come as a bit of a surprise. I think it's a pretty accurate representation of what the disciples were like when Jesus first chose them, which gives me great encouragement that He could choose *me* too.

If you have been a Christian longer than a few weeks, you qualify for this first disciple-making behavior: prayer. The prayer-question is: *who do You want me to invest in, Lord?*

Why ask God this question? Why not just answer the question yourself? Because you don't know you or your potential candidates very well whereas God does. Jesus, you remember, had already called several of the twelve to His side. But by the time He needed to formalize the exact persons whom He was to designate "apostles," as Mark puts it, there was a large crowd following Him. The selection of those exact persons was what drove Him to that full night of prayer. Remember also that He said "the Son can do nothing by himself; he can only do what he sees his Father doing" (John 5:19). Jesus felt Himself inadequate to make the selection. He trusted that the Father knew precisely whom to select.

In the same way, the Lord knows who He wants you to invest in. And, He knows how to tell you, if you ask. In my case, I was chatting with John Wimber between sessions at a conference he was leading in the early 80's. Suddenly John's face changed and he looked with at me with a piercing look for a couple of seconds. Then he said, "How would you like to go with me to a conference I'm leading in Ft. Worth in a couple of weeks?" God said, "OK," and I began a discipling relationship with John that changed my ministry. God had spoken to John about me and John responded with that invitation.

PROTECTION. Another focus of Jesus' prayer for the disciples was their protection. This is a spiritual world and the primary dynamic occurring on the surface of this planet is spiritual warfare. The longest prayer which scripture records Jesus praying—John 17— shows Jesus praying for the protection of His disciples *three* times! There are black hats and white hats out there, and we must be responsible for seeing that Jesus' disciples are covered with the Lord's protection until they learn to do so for themselves.

I say things like this: "Lord, build a new hedge around George today. Protect him from temptation, accusation, deception, and harassment. Protect his family, his home, his job, and his transportation. Keep him safe from all the enemy's stratagems."

UNITY. A third focus of praying for disciples is their unity. Jesus was always having to deal with His disciples' *dis*unity, expressed especially in their competitiveness with one another. Their unity, He prayed in John 17, would be the sign of the Incarnation to the world: "May they be brought to complete unity to let the world know that you sent me and have loved them even as you have loved me" (v.23). There is much to divide Christians: doctrines, immaturity, poor attitudes, feelings of insecurity, self-rejection, pride, misunderstanding and the like *ad nauseam*. These, note, are not disqualifiers from discipling; rather they are concerns to take to the Lord in prayer and to disciples in grace.

We need to be praying that those we are

discipling will be motivated to understand and maintain the attitudes and actions that make for unity.

2

He Recruited Them

"Follow me"
Matthew 9:9

It's not enough, of course, to find out who you're supposed to select for discipling. You have to tell them. Then they must exercise their free wills and accept or reject your selection. Some whom Jesus selected refused the offer, as in the case of the rich young ruler (Matthew 19:16-24). Most accepted.

BEHAVIOR: HE RECRUITED THEM
FOCUS: CALLING

Calling is a dynamic that has been around the Christian church for a long time. It is an awareness that God is assigning a particular role to a believer. It is important to remember that God calls and we recruit. Only God knows the natural and spiritual abilities He has deposited in someone's life; only He knows the direction He wants his follower to go in living out those abilities; only He knows the unique twists and turns which his follower's path will take.

Jesus' call on people was sometimes stated right at the outset: "I will make you fishers of men," "you will see heaven open, and the angels of God ascending and descending on the Son of Man," "you are Simon" (a reed); "you will be called Cephas" (a rock; that is, there will be a real personality change).

At other times He gave no end-point to the call, simply saying, "follow me," as to Levi. That was enough for Levi (Matthew), who was probably ripping off the citizens by inflating their tax bills. Just to follow Jesus was itself a major call to change his life.

To announce the end-point is daunting for some people. Maybe it's best not to tell them much about where you think they're headed. Others may need to see something of the goal in order to be able to respond to the invitation to be discipled. Be flexible and look to the Lord for direction.

God calls. But we recruit. I have rarely been refused in my invitation to disciple someone. God has gotten there first, placing a desire for growth or ministry or responsibility in their hearts. It's very confirming for both them and me to realize that God has been at work on them through themselves and others and, now, through me as well.

Then, our job is to try to discern the work of God in them and their heart for serving by asking them certain questions:

- what are your natural abilities and

inclinations?

• what are your spiritual gifts? Are they enhancements of your natural abilities or do they operate in brand new areas for you?

• what kinds of needs draw your heart to do something about them?

• whose ministry do you admire and want to emulate?

• if you had your heart's desire, what would you do for the kingdom of God?

Now nobody, not even St. Paul, springs full-grown into ministry and maturity. No matter what the end result for them that God foresees, they have to start at a starting point. As a discipler, you can greatly assist by helping them look around for an opportunity to serve. "He who is faithful in small things will be given larger things," Jesus said, so it's no slight to them to suggest a humble beginning.

I think that the first ministry role Jesus gave his disciples was, in modern terms, ushering. They helped people know where to sit (in groups of 50 when the 5,000 were fed, for example). They probably orchestrated the presentation of sick people to Jesus. They went on errands. Earth-shaking stuff? No. Not at the beginning.

What are the things that need to be done at your church? The initial stages of discipling release man-hours for the needs of the organization while they provide the entry point for fledgling followers of Jesus. Ushering, setting up tables and chairs, collating materials, teaching Sunday School, directing traffic, vacuuming, cooking and serving, running errands, passing out supplies, gardening. If your disciple is too big to do such things, he or she is too small to be a disciple of Jesus Christ.

Once your disciples have proved that they have a heart for serving others, natural enlargements of their responsibilities will suggest themselves. A disciple who starts out as an usher at an adult class may, for example, become a researcher of materials and then a sometime presenter and finally the class teacher.

You might think of the starting point as the center of a circle. As you think about and converse with your disciple, which direction towards the outside of the circle seems appropriate? There's lots of directions possible from the center of a circle. Will you aim him or her in the direction of leadership or administration or teaching or helps or ministries of mercy or healing or counseling or prayer? And what is the next step? What thing can they put their hands to now which will prove their heart for service and give them a taste of the area they're interested in?

Spend time with your disciple talking about these things. Encourage them to dream. If they don't know what they are to do, take them with you while you do some things. Let them side-kick with you. They may just need to see real ministry going on in order to get something of a vision for what ministry is all about.

Help them price out discipling. Jesus said to count the cost. The expendables are time, energy, and money. Help them get some understanding of what discipling is going to cost in these three factors. Also, when John Wimber invited me to accompany him to Texas, I was unable to afford the costs of the trip. When I told him, John said, "That's OK, I'll pay for it." That is, it also costs *us* to invest in disciples for Jesus. Are you willing to pay that price?

Share your own story with them. How did you get into ministry? Who helped you? What was it like at the beginning? How did you feel about it? Do you recall any significant turning points in your development? The ones you're discipling may need to see your journey in some detail before they have the courage or vision or model to enable them to respond.

3

He Hung Out With Them

"He appointed twelve . . . that they might be with him."
Mark 3:14

If you get out a detailed map of the Holy Land and plot some of the journeys that Jesus took with his disciples, you'll soon realize that He spent huge amounts of time with them alone, privately, apart from the crowds. Most of those retreat trips took at least two weeks. Overall, I think it is easy to demonstrate that He spent *half* of his time with the twelve alone, and the other half with the twelve in the presence of the public. He was almost always with the twelve; He was sometimes with the public as well.

I might now ask you two obvious questions: 1) who is your public? 2) who are your disciples? Your public might be a Sunday School class or the poor to whom you distribute food or the Bible study group that meets in your house or your congregation—if you are a pastor—or the neighbors you are witnessing to or the ladies guild or the youth group. That's your public. But your disciples are those you are recruiting to be involved in an intentional, intense, investing of up to half of your available time, energy, and money.

BEHAVIOR: HE HUNG OUT WITH THEM
FOCUS: FRIENDSHIP

If you could climb into a time machine and go back to the three years Jesus spent with the disciples, I think you'd be astounded at how much time Jesus wasted with them. A lot of the time, there was no particular agenda. That is, it was not an achievement-focused but a relation-ship-focused thing that was going on. What Jesus was making out of them was friends. If He made disciples without making them friends, they'd have been drastically deficient announcers of the Gospel. Not all friends need become disciples, but every disciple needs to become a friend.

Friendship takes time. It's one of the things that God seems determined *not* to speed up with the aid of spiritual gifts and divine power. He'll divinely speed up lots of others things, but not friendship. There's simply no substitute for the expenditure of large amounts of time in the making of friends. Love, someone observed, is spelled T-I-M-E. We spend time with those we love. If we're not spending time with them, there's a real question about the nature of our relationship with them. It may be informational or neighborly or structural, but the relationship will not be friend-making without the expenditure of time. Lot's of it.

You can't always be accomplishing something—except friend-making—in the time spent. Let's say that God wants you to spend four hours a week with your disciple. Who can study the Bible for that whole time? or teach classes? or pray for the sick? or any *thing* else? No, considerable time just needs to be spent without any other agenda than to spend time together.

What is it that makes for friendship?

Attraction
There must be something attractive about those we spend time with. A common interest or hobby or pursuit. An affinity of some kind—something which binds you together. A wanting to be like one another.

Mutuality
An ability to give and receive from one another.

Enjoyment
Liking to be in one another's company.

Understanding
Growing in your understanding of one another's motives, perspectives, beliefs, relationships, patterns, and goals. Eventually being able to speak for one another in the other's absence.

Knowledge
There must be a large exchange of information about one another.

Challenge
Iron sharpens iron, as the old truism goes.

Vulnerability
Friends expose themselves to one another, thereby giving one another leverage on each other. If friends can't trust one another to use

information about one another wisely, they won't become real friends.

Proximity

It's difficult to develop friendship with someone you can't be around on a regular basis. Even pen-pals need to see each other's faces now and again.

A great way to begin sharing with each other on a quality level is to share each other's histories. One way to do that is to draw a line across the middle of a sheet of paper, labeling the left edge "birth" and the right edge "today". Along that line write dates, key events, people, ups and downs, happy faces and sad faces, and other stuff like that. Then share for at least an hour, interviewing each other about your histories, probing for more knowledge and understanding.

Probably one of the best ways to spend time together is to eat together. (Someone pointed out that the Gospel of Luke acts most of itself out on the stage of seven meals.) Eating, by itself, is no guarantee that discipling will occur, but it's a great atmosphere in which to become friends. And at the beginning, I wouldn't try to load the meal down with extra agendas, except to get to know each other. Later, you might utilize inductive Bible study materials or tackle problems or pray about needs, but at the beginning, I'd just make friends by becoming thoroughly acquainted with each other.

By the way, a discipling relationship is not a professional relationship. Today, professionals are taught to be impersonal, unemotional, uninvolved, even aloof. But it is clear from the

Gospels that Jesus exposed his inmost thoughts and feelings to his disciples. They knew what He thought about life, the Pharisees, governments, God, the church and marriage because He clearly told them. They knew when He was angry, frustrated, sad, worried, amazed, and happy because He openly expressed these feelings. He was no stick figure, imperviously gliding across the surface of the planet. Rather He was real, involved, vulnerable, honest, especially in relationship with his disciples. They saw him weep, they heard him moan.

Your disciples need to see your reality. There's a stream of thought in the minds of most followers that their leaders somehow have something extra going for them by virtue of education or ordination or position or age or experience. This assumption allows them to dismiss your successes and their failures in walking with the Lord because you have that something extra. For the sake of their growth—and yours!—you need to debunk that myth. How are they going to appreciate your success in resisting temptation if they never hear of failures? How will they ever get a vision and a hope for their own growth if they never hear of your actual struggles? You must deplasticize yourself or they will hold unrealistic opinions of what it takes to walk the talk.

Are you willing to be vulnerable with them?[1]

I often confessed my sins from the pulpit, but I would only confess past sins, sins that I had already gained victory over. One day I got more honest and mentioned a current sin. Afterwards a man in my congregation came up to me and said, "Thank God that you confessed a current sin today! I had the idea that you only had past sins, which disheartened me about my prospects of victory over present sins in my life." That was one small factor which helped him grow in his relationship with Jesus. Last I heard, he had just helped plant a church on his vacation in the former Soviet Union.

Your vulnerability begets theirs. Do you want plastic disciples? No? Then you'd better not be plastic around them. Befriend them. Friends are real with each other.

4

He Taught Them

> *"He taught them many things by parables."* Mark 4:2

One of Jesus' titles among his followers was "teacher." Obviously He spent considerable time teaching them. Sometimes the teaching was a formal lecture, sometimes a response to a question.

BEHAVIOR: HE TAUGHT THEM
FOCUS: REALITY, BOUNDARY-DEFINITION

The sermon on the mount was a formal setting-forth of information about life. At other times, He taught his disciples on the run.

Disciplers are presented with a bit of a problem here, for scripture warns, "not many of you should presume to be teachers, my brothers, because you know that we who teach will be judged more strictly" (James 3:1). God means for teachers to be listened to. That's why they will be judged more strictly, for they are meant to be heard and they better teach only what's right. In my experience, few people have the gift of teaching. So what's a discipler to do who doesn't have the gift of teaching?

One thing is to get your disciples to those who do have the gift of teaching. Recommend trustworthy books and articles and Bible study materials to them. Take them to events where Godly teachers will be ministering.

Whether or not you have the gift of teaching, you can still perform many of the functions of teaching if you recognize what they are. Almost always when Jesus taught—both the twelve and the public—He taught about the Kingdom of God. That is to say, He kept describing "the big picture." Here's what life is about, He'd say, a sower went out to sow his seed ... a man found a pearl of great value ... a king was settling accounts ... the third was given one talent. Here's what the playing field of life looks like, He'd say, here are the ways to get along, these are the principles you need to live out, here are the priorities which are really important, this is what to believe and what not to believe.

The Kingdom of God is about the reign of God. Jesus taught about God as the King, He taught about Satan as the usurper, He taught about God's power and how it is meant to work, He taught about reward and punishment, He taught about how to relate with God and with Jesus and with family and with believers and with unbelievers. He taught on the big picture. Again and again. Over and over. In large print and in small print. In other words, He taught the main and the plain.

That's what you can do for your disciples. You can keep the big picture of a big God before them. The big picture will give them perspective, values, faith, and wisdom. It will provide the principles by which to make decisions. It will sustain them in times of trial or difficulty. It will give them goals. It will land them in heaven.

Another of the functions you can do for your disciples is illustrate teachings by your own life. Mother birds gather and predigest worms in order to regurgitate them in the gullets of their babies. A teacher predigests the Word of God by living it out, proving that it works, and then feeding it to his students. What passages, what truths in scripture mean something real to you? How did you discover those truths? What challenge from the Bible came your way? How did you respond to that challenge? What happened? How did it turn out? What did God do for you as you met that challenge?

You see, you have real authority to teach those parts of the Word which you have proven in your own life. If you haven't proven it in your own life, it's just a theory to you, isn't it. Maybe a nice Biblical theory, but a theory nonetheless until it's lived out. People need to see truth incarnated. When something in the Word has become real in you, it gives others hope that they, too, can profitably live out the Word in their own lives.

What in the Word of God have you lived out, even if imperfectly? Teach that! If your disciple needs a truth you haven't yet lived, do it together, or get him to someone who has lived out that truth.

Want some examples? Take a look at these commands from Jesus in Matthew and see which ones you have put into action:

• "Repent, for the kingdom of heaven is near." 4:17. Have you done that? When? How? What happened? What's been the result?

• "Do not resist an evil person?" 5:39. Do you know what that means? Have you found out what it means by doing what He said?

• "Ask and it will be given to you; seek and you will find; knock and the door will be opened to you." 7:7. What is something you've gotten because you persisted in asking for it?

• "But go and learn what this means: 'I desire mercy, not sacrifice.'" 9:13.

• "Do not be afraid; you are worth more than many sparrows." 10:31

• "But what was sown on good soil is the man who hears the word and understands it.
He produces a crop, yielding a hundred, sixty, or thirty times what was sown." 13:23.

• "Be on your guard against the yeast of the Pharisees and Sadducees." 16:6. Why did Jesus think the influence of those parties was so important to resist?

• "See that you do not look down on one of these little ones." 18:10.

• "For I was hungry and you gave me something to eat, I was thirsty and you gave me something to drink, I was a stranger and you invited me in, I needed clothes and you clothed me, I was sick and you looked after me, I was in prison and you came to visit me." 25:35-36. Have you done any of those six things? Which? What benefit came to you because of obeying these commands?

Or, have you dodged any commands that Jesus has tried to get you to act on? Which? What's been the result of side-stepping his Word? What have you learned from that? Would you be willing to share that learning with your disciple?

If I were to tell you that *obedience precedes understanding,* would you know by your own experience what that means? Have you ever done something Jesus commanded even though you did not understand why it was important to do it? What command? What was the outcome? How would you express what you now understand?

These are the things that teachers pour into the minds and hearts of their disciples.

√√√

OK. We've seen so far that Jesus engaged in four intentional behaviors by way of making disciples. He prayed for them, recruited them, hung out with them, and taught them. There are three left.

5

He Apprenticed Them

> "He sent them
> out to preach the
> kingdom of God
> and to heal the sick."
> Luke 9:2

It was important that the disciples learn *how* to conduct their ministries. Jesus didn't just send them out to do a job without giving them specific training in how to do that job.

BEHAVIOR: HE CONDUCTED A MASTER-APPRENTICE RELATIONSHIP WITH THEM
FOCUS: SKILL DEVELOPMENT

In God the Father's plan for Jesus, it seems to me to be a key that He was born into the home of a tradesman. I've talked to a lot of tradesmen. They understand apprenticing. They realize how a skill is transferred from one person to another. They realize that it is a slow, careful process.

When Joseph was making a carpenter out of his son, that son was learning the steps by which to impart skills to others. My Dad was a tradesman, a machinist. He was also a fisherman. When I was a youngster, my Dad apprenticed me in the art—the skill—of fishing. But first, he taught me how to make go-getters. A go-getter is a lure that is especially appealing to crappies, a bluegill type of freshwater fish. Here are the steps:

1. He did it.
My Dad manufactured the lures in our garage.

2. He did it and I watched.
I went out into the garage and watched him take expended .22 shell casings and put them in the vice. He then drilled a small hole through the casing, near the base. Then to provide an eye to tie fishing line to, he put a small cotter pin through the hole, prying the ends around the casing to lock it in place. Then he put red finger-nail polish down inside the casing. He then tied a long-shaft hook and a bundle of white feathers together and stuck them down the casing into the polish, which then dried. Finally he painted half the outside of the casing with more red polish.

3. He did it and I helped.
He let me place the casings in the vice. He let me insert the drill bit into the drill and tighten it. He let me hand him new casings when he was done with the old ones. He let me cut the feathers to the right length and hand them with the hook to him in preparation for tying.
He let me paint some casings on my own.

4. I did it and he helped.
He put his hands on mine as I held the drill and tried to drill the holes. He let me take the pliers and insert the cotter pin through the hole, correcting me when I inserted it crooked. He helped me tie the hook and feathers together, showing me how tightly to wrap the tie-line around them. He held my hands in his as I poured the polish into the casing, showing me by the pressure of his hands when I had poured enough. He helped me design the final coating of polish on the outside of the casing.

5. I did it and he watched.
He let me drill the holes when he thought I could hold the drill steady. He watched me push the cotter pin through the hole. He let me tie the hook and the feathers together, being sure that the tie was tight and secure. He let me pour the red fingernail polish down into the casing. He let me insert the hook-and-feathers into the casing, cementing them in the base with the polish.

6. I did it and he mentored me as needed.
From that point on, in preparation for a fishing trip, I could make go-getters when he was at work. He inspected them when he got home, offering correction or commendation as appropriate.

When we got to Rodriguez Lake in Baja California, I learned how to fish, using those go-getters, in the same six-step process. I learned how to catch many crappies.

This is how skill is transmitted.

What do *you* know how to do? Don't just think of "spiritual" things. What skills have been transmitted to you—business skills, construction skills, artistic or creative skills, fabricating skills, relational skills, selling skills, driving-cooking-instrument playing-instrument using-electrical-sewing-painting-gardening skills? What have you taught yourself how to do? Listen now: *any* legitimate skill you can teach another will benefit the world and the kingdom of God.

Even if the skill you transmit has nothing to do with spiritual things, the *process* of apprenticing another will itself be used by God to form him as a disciple. Jesus could teach his followers how to catch men because he had been taught by his father how to make plows. Discipleship slides laterally quite easily. If you've been apprenticed in one skill, you'll find it easier to be apprenticed in others.

Then, do you know any spiritual skills? Have you learned something about how to collaborate with God and man for the kingdom's benefit? In my case, my range of skills is pretty narrow. I know how to put on conferences in which the leadership listens effectively to God, follows His leads, builds unified teams, takes appropriate action, sees the power of God released, apprentices people in several levels of skill (such as one-on-one ministry, master-apprenticing, teaching, etc.), responds effectively to the unforeseen (either from people or the Spirit or from the devil), keeps one's balance, gives the glory to God, and gets out. I don't know a lot, but I know how to do that. So I do it with vigor. I've led conferences in which I've taught and ministered in over 800 sessions, I've discipled more than 1000 team members in various levels of skill, I've seen thousands healed of various physical and emotional ailments, and God has used me to build up leadership. You wanna learn how to do conferences, come and see me.

How did I learn how to lead conferences? For a year, I followed John Wimber around while he did conferences. I went with him on four weekends and a two-week event. I watched what he did and I helped as best I could. In that year I was given enough understanding of the skill of conference-leading that I could go out and do conferences myself. The Lord took me by the hand and guided me into conferences which I was "up for." As I did them, I learned more. Pretty soon, I could apprentice others. Since that year, I've done conferences for over a decade.

Sometime get out your Bible and compare how Jesus raised Jairus' daughter from the dead (Matthew 9) and how Peter—who was present in Jairus' house—raised Dorcas from the dead (Acts 9). As you compare them, ask yourself: what did Jesus do? and what did Peter do? Compare their behaviors. Even in something so monumental as raising the dead, there are skills to be learned. Hello? Peter wasn't operating in a vacuum. He simply mimicked what he had seen Jesus do. It worked for Jesus. And it worked for Peter.

6

He Debriefed Them

"What were you arguing about on the road?"
Mark 9:33

A teacher once told me that people don't learn from experience. This seemed odd to me, for I thought that they did. But the teacher went on: "people don't learn from experience; they learn from *reflecting* on experience." That made sense. I've seen people make the same mistake over and over, not yet learning from their experiences. But when people reflect on, think about, examine, and ponder their experiences, they can learn a great deal from them

BEHAVIOR: HE DEBRIEFED THEM
FOCUS: CHARACTER DEVELOPMENT, SKILL ENHANCEMENT

CHARACTER. When Jesus was hanging out with the disciples, they often provided grist for the learning mill. All He had to do was keep his eyes open and wait, and, sure enough, they would do something which would cause him to comment. A great percentage of what Jesus taught them was in response to their actions.

For example, there they are following him along the road on the way home to Capernaum. When they get inside, He turns and asks, "What were you arguing about on the road?" Their response is silence. His just asking the question is enough to put the finger on something they need to deal with. What is that? Pride. They had been competing with each other for greatness.

Do you know how often they argued over which of them was the greatest? Not once. Not twice. Not three times. Luke's Gospel states that they were still indulging in this argument *at the Last Supper!* These turkeys were consistently dense students over this matter. They didn't learn the first time Jesus corrected them. Nor the second. Nor the third. Finally, as I referenced earlier, their denseness forced him at the last supper to end this eternal jockeying for position by taking the role of a slave himself.

Now, there's a bit of comfort for you here. Are you disappointed at how long it is taking you to learn something of the character of a follower of Jesus? Take heart! The very twelve that He himself selected were all clods! Their sin was the worst of all: spiritual pride. As dense, as self-centered, as sinful as they were, He selected them and stuck with them all through their immaturity. He'll do the same for you.

Jesus didn't just debrief them on negative things. He also commented on the positive: He exclaimed that Nathaniel was a man without guile; when Peter confessed Him as the Savior, He replied, "good for you, Peter."

One of the things I've learned about selecting people for positions of leadership is to choose for character over giftedness. If there are two candidates for the job, I'll choose the one with the strongest character rather than the strongest gifts. Why? Well, it's best summarized in a quote by E. M. Bounds: "The church is always looking for better methods, but God is always looking for better people; people *are* God's method." Who you are is God's handiwork and who you are is his gift to others even more than what you can do.

If you can't yet handle opposition or conflict maturely but are wonderfully able to heal the sick, I'll still put someone who has demonstrated an ability to handle conflict maturely in the job instead of you, even if his gifts are paltry in comparison with yours. What good is it to heal the sick if they get alienated and leave? The health of their souls is more important than the health of their bodies.

There is a passage in Luke 14 that we must look at here, because it is a major disqualifier of potential disciples. "If anyone comes to me and does not hate his father and mother, his wife and children, his brothers and sisters—yes, even his own life—*he cannot be my disciple.* And anyone who does not carry his cross and follow me *cannot be my disciple*" (vv. 26-27, my italics). Jesus puts his finger squarely on the matter of priority here: "Am I first in your life or is anything else first?"

About twenty years ago I approached my wife rather tentatively and said, "I feel I must tell you that you're no longer in first place in my life, for I have to give that position to Jesus." Sue just nodded that she had received the message, but said nothing. After a few weeks, however, she came to me and said, "You know when you told me I was now in second place?"

"Yes," I answered.

"Well, I want you to know that second place now is better than first place used to be!" The principle here is gain-through-loss. It's one of the areas where Jesus turns our world's values absolutely upside down. The way to get ahead is to lose: your life, your wants, your self-determination, your agenda, your everything.

Most mornings I take a prayer-walk. First thing I say is: "I sign myself with the sign of the cross, and I mean to deny myself, take up my cross today, and follow you, Lord, for I want to be your disciple more than anything else." Often I have to confess that I have failed, followed by a fresh appropriation of his forgiveness. By these criteria, I am not yet a complete disciple. But I am on the path and I'm not stepping off it, no matter how many failures mock my intent. For Jesus has crooked his little finger at me and I am going to go on going on in my attempts to follow him.

Can you say, "I want to follow you, Lord"? If not that, can you say, "I want to want to follow you, Lord"? If not that, can you say, "I want to want to want to follow you, Lord"? He will meet you and begin to work with you *wherever* you are. Without his help you cannot carry your cross, and without carrying your cross you cannot be his disciple. In his partnership with you, your role is intent, his role is ability.

The Greek word "character" means the imprint of a signet ring on clay. A disciple of Jesus receives and shows forth his imprint more and more.

SKILL ENHANCEMENT. The second focus of Jesus' practice of debriefing the disciples was the enhancement of their skills. He had already developed their skills through the master-apprentice model, but here He enhanced their skills through debriefing. For instance, the disciples were trying to minister to a demonized boy while Jesus was off on the mountain getting transfigured. They weren't having any success.

Boy, I can really identify with them. The first time I ran into a real demon, nothing I tried succeeded in getting that thing out. It was very discouraging. There was a reason why that demon wasn't budging on my say so. Finally I had to check in with Jesus and get His input. Then I finally saw what was needed and remedied my approach. The spirit then left. In essence, Jesus had debriefed me in the middle of the episode.

The disciples didn't have the benefit of His presence in the middle of this failure, but He arrived shortly after. When the father of the demonized boy told Jesus the story—including the disciples' failure to get rid of it—Jesus responded with a fairly weighty rebuke calling them an "unbelieving and perverse generation" and wondering out loud "how long shall I put up with you?" Matthew 17:17.

So the first part of His debriefing of them was a rebuke. Later, after He had cast out the demon and they had gone indoors, they pursued the matter, "Why couldn't we drive it out?" He replied, "Because you have so little faith. I tell you the truth, if you have faith as small as a mustard seed, you can say to this mountain, 'Move from here to there' and it will move. Nothing will be impossible for you." I wrote a book on faith entitled The Mustard Seed Book, and I don't want to do an in depth treatment of having faith here. I just want to say that the having of faith is a skill. Jesus had demonstrated that skill of faith over and over for them and was a bit peeved that they hadn't yet got the message.

Mark's version of this story elaborates on the faith-skill in which they had proved deficient. When they asked why they couldn't drive it out, He replied, "This kind can come out only by prayer" (Mark 9:29). There are all sorts of prayer. Usually in a case of demonization the kind of prayer needed is a prayer of command: "get out!" But in this instance, Jesus seemed to be saying that the one to talk to was God, not the demon. Why? I don't know. My guess is that some demons are stronger than others and that when they're strong, the appropriate thing to do is ask the Lord for greater power to deal with them.

In any event, Jesus seemed to think the disciples could have handled the situation themselves. His debriefing of their experience identified the source of their failure: lack of faith and appropriate prayer. He went on to encourage them by saying that the smallest amount of the real thing was enough for the biggest job. (Palestine mustard seeds are the merest sliver of organic matter.)

Let me mention one more key thing about Jesus here. He could say pretty harsh things to the disciples and they still stuck around. They didn't get wounded and go off and sulk over his rebukes. Why? I think it was because they knew that He loved and accepted them. Love and acceptance come first: they provide the foundation to stand on when the disciples need a correction. If I know you love and accept me, I can take any correction because I know the thing I did wrong doesn't disqualify me from your love or acceptance.

7

He Anointed Them

> *"I have given you
> authority to trample on
> snakes and scorpions
> and to overcome all
> the power of the
> enemy."*
> *Luke 10:19*

FOCUS: SPIRITUAL EMPOWERMENT

"Anointing" is a key biblical word which
nonetheless remains a rather mysterious matter.
In both the Hebrew in which the Old Testament
was written and the Greek in which the New
Testament was written, the words describing Jesus
(Messiah and Christ) mean "anointed one." In
fact, to be a Christian means to be an anointed
one. When prophets in Old Testament times
made someone a king, they "anointed" him. St.
John says to Christians, "you have an anointing
from the Holy One" (I John 2:20). That is, there
is a general anointing that every Christian

possesses. But what about anointings for ministry? That's more particularized.

What is an anointing and how do you get one? An anointing is a transference of power, an impartation of an enablement, which makes one a conduit through which the power and authority of God can flow. A person cannot act in an anointing without the immediate cooperation of the Spirit of God.

An anointing is what is being talked about in this passage from Luke: "When Jesus had called the twelve together, he gave them power and authority to drive out all demons and to cure diseases, and he sent them out to preach the kingdom of God and to heal the sick" (9:1-2). They were at the sixth stage of the master-apprentice relationship: they did it and he monitored them. In other words, they were to be on their own for a time, ministering under Jesus' training and authority. The thing they yet lacked He now gave them: an anointing. The anointing He gave them centered on two things: the ability to do works of power and the ability to speak effectively. He gave them his empowerment, his anointing to do these things.

"When they returned, they reported to Jesus what they had done. Then he took them with him and they withdrew by themselves" (9:10). (You see that what He's trying to do now is debrief them on the experiences they had on their ministry trip.)

The Bible doesn't tell us *how* Jesus anointed them, just that He did. In the very next chapter of Luke, we see that He did it again, this time with seventy-two others. "After this the Lord appointed seventy-two others and sent them two by two ahead of him to every town and place where he was about to go. ... Heal the sick who are there and tell them, 'The kingdom of God is near you.'" (Luke 10: 1, 9). When they returned, they also reported on their success, and Jesus repeated the message about his anointing, "I have given you authority to trample on snakes and scorpions and to overcome all the power of the enemy; nothing will harm you" (v.19).

Again, the anointing had two parts: the ability to exercise God's power and the ability to proclaim His word effectively. Jesus wasn't about to send his troops out to do something He hadn't empowered them to do. Was the anointing, then, sort of magical, operating automatically on its own? No, it is clear from Scripture that the disciples had to blend their faith and their maturity with the anointing in order for it to be effective. But it is also clear that they couldn't be effective without it.

If we look closely at the end of each of the four gospels, we see that each of them contains a version of the Great Commission. And each commission contains two parts: a power part and a word part[2].

The power part	The word part
Matthew: power is Jesus' authority given, by implication, to his followers: "All authority in heaven and on earth has been given to me. Therefore go and make disciples"	The word focuses on teaching: "Teach them to obey everything I have commanded you."
Mark: power is accompanying signs: "And these signs will accompany those who believe."	The word is: "Go into all the world and preach the good news to all creation."
Luke: power is a prerequisite for service: "I am going to send you what my Father has promised; but stay in the city until you have been clothed with power from on high."	The word is: "repentance and forgiveness of sins will be preached in his name to all nations, beginning at Jerusalem."
John: power is for the forgiving or retaining of sins: "Receive the Holy Spirit. If you forgive anyone his sins, they are forgiven; if you do not forgive them, they are not forgiven."	The word is being sent in the same fashion as Jesus was sent: "*As* the Father has sent me, I am sending you" (my italics).

These two parts of each version of the Great Commission reflect the two central parts of Jesus' empowerment of his disciples: doing and speaking. In other words, the same tasks that Jesus commanded the disciples to do are those He commands us to do; and the same anointing that was available to the disciples is available to us.

Now, how does one get anointed? Let me borrow excerpts from a couple of pages in a book I wrote earlier with my friend, Doug Gregg:

> Jesus' last will and testament, if we might use that phrase, is found in the first paragraphs of Acts. Jesus was about to return to the Father, and here he gives final instructions to his disciples. While eating with them, he said, "Do not leave Jerusalem, but wait for the gift my Father promised, which you have heard me speak about. For John baptized with water, but in a few days you will be baptized with the Holy Spirit" (1:4b-5).
>
> The disciples seemed to be interested in eschatological (end-time) matters, but Jesus directed them back again to what he considered crucial: "It is not for you to know the times or dates the Father has set by his own authority. But you will receive power when the Holy Spirit comes on you; and you will be my witnesses in Jerusalem, and in all Judea and Samaria, and to the ends of the earth." Those are Jesus' last recorded

words before his ascension back into
heaven.

Notice that what the disciples had
seen and heard of Jesus up to this point
was not yet enough to equip them for
effective ministry. They had been in his
company for three years. They had seen
all the healings and miracles. They had
heard all the teachings. they had even
gone out on limited missions and had
themselves preached with power, healed
the sick and cast out demons (Matthew
10; Luke 9). They had watched Jesus die
and they had touched his risen body.
Why were they yet unready for their
ministries? What did they still lack?

What they lacked is indicated in
Jesus' prediction, "You will receive power
when the Holy Spirit comes on you"
(Acts 1:8). Hadn't they had power when
they went out on mission? Yes, they had,
but apparently it was of a limited nature
and duration; now it was to be replaced
by a more extensive and permanent
empowerment. The disciples pre-
Pentecost experience seems similar to
that of Old Testament figures on whom
the Spirit came for certain purposes, only
to leave them after those purposes were
fulfilled.

This is in no way to state that the
disciples didn't already have the Holy
Spirit in them. Every believer has the
Holy Spirit within. ...

Nonetheless, Jesus seems to have

thought that in some sense the Spirit was not yet on them, or was not yet in them in *fullness*....

It won't do to get very dogmatic about how the empowering of the Spirit occurs. In the book of Acts there are at least five different ways or sequences in which it happens. ...

The scriptural record urges me to hold to the need for empowerment. But I am extremely reluctant to say that it must occur in some particular order or method or style. I know this much: it takes God's power to do God's work. God works through people, yes, but he insists that his power, not ours, be the energizing force of that work....

My observation is that the Spirit interacts with us at successive levels or stages. I personally have experienced four major demarcations occurring in 1972 (in-filling), 1974 (anointing for inner healing), 1983 (exposure to power ministry), and 1990 (heightened commitment to prayer). Each of these levels of interaction with the Spirit renewed and refreshed me and brought significantly greater effectiveness to my ministry. It thrills me to wonder what's coming next, for as the riches of Christ are past searching out, so the ministries of the Spirit must be inexhaustible. (Inner Healing, Inter Varsity Press. 1993 pp. 159-162).

So, we must ourselves be empowered by the Holy Spirit, and we must see that our disciples become empowered also. This brings up two agendas:

1) If you are not yet empowered by the Holy Spirit, I encourage you to find someone you know who is, and ask him or her to pray for you, laying claim to Jesus' promise, to "baptize you with the Holy Spirit." Jesus is the only Baptizer in the Spirit, so He alone can do it for you. Let your friend ask Jesus to fill you with the Spirit.

2) If your disciple is not yet empowered by the Holy Spirit, study with him the beginnings of each of the gospels where John the Baptist predicts that Jesus will baptize people with the Holy Spirit. Review the four versions of the Great Commission. Look at the 1st, 2nd, 8th, 9th, 10th, and 19th chapters of the Book of Acts to see how the early followers of Jesus were empowered by the Holy Spirit. Then simply ask Jesus to baptize your friend with his Holy Spirit.

After a person has been prayed with to be baptized in the Holy Spirit, he should try his hand at many situations requiring the power of the Spirit and see what happens. Sometimes the Lord will give specific direction to someone while they are being filled—or sometime after—concerning the nature of the ministry they are to exercise. That's what happened to me in 1983. But you know what? I already knew that a good bit of my anointing was for healing because I had experimented with praying for the sick. In fact, through trial and error, I found out that my particular anointing was for the healing of joints.

Almost everyone I prayed for with joint problems—arthritis, bursitis, bone spurs, scoliosis, etc.—was healed to some significant degree.

Your disciple's gifting may be any combination of the gifts—or parts of gifts—mentioned in the Bible. For example, my gift-pak runs something like this: 50% teaching, 10% healing, 10% encouraging, 30% leading. What would you say yours is? The Bible's lists of gifts contain these items: Romans 12: prophesying, serving, teaching, encouraging, giving, leadership, showing mercy; 1 Corinthians 12: the word of wisdom, the word of knowledge, faith, gifts of healings, miraculous powers, prophecy, the discernment of spirits, speaking in tongues, interpretation of tongues; Ephesians 4: apostles, prophets, evangelists, pastors, and teachers; 1 Peter 4: speaking and serving.

Anointings are raw material which have to be experimented with, educated, trained, corrected, and guarded—all of which can be provided by other people. But the raw material itself, the anointing, can only be given by the Holy Spirit.

Conclusion

*"Take care of
my sheep."*
John 21:16

YOU, THE DISCIPLER

I believe that each ministry, in Jesus' mind, has 2 parts: 1) to do the ministry, 2) to train someone else to do it. As you gain a bit of proficiency in a ministry, quickly look for opportunities to train someone else in it. You can't train them in what you don't yet know, but you can train them in what you do know. You only have to know *some*thing they don't know in order to train them; you don't have to know *every*thing they don't know.

I have a wonderful response to the dreaded question about something I don't know. The response is, "I don't know." It is always an acceptable answer.

Only Jesus was perfectly competent in all seven of the methods by which He made disciples out of his followers. He is still capable of perfect competence, some of which He chooses to administer through you. As you glance back over this brief book, which of the seven behaviors seems most to beckon you? Let me restate them as though you are the one to achieve them:

1. I pray for them.
2. I recruit them.
3. I hang out with them.
4. I teach them.
5. I apprentice them.
6. I debrief them.
7. I see that they get anointed.

My particular package of these counts out like this in time expenditure: pray 10%, recruit 2%, hang out 15%, teach 40%, apprentice 15%, debrief 10%, anoint 8%. Notice that I don't do some of these things very much or very well. Hanging out, for instance; I'm pretty introverted. But I can do what I can do. And Jesus can get the rest of it done through others.

As you look at the following questionnaire, think about yourself and respond according to what the Lord has deposited in you by way of interest, ability, and experience.

QUESTIONNAIRE

1. <u>I pray for them</u>. I have a special urging inside to pray for those God wants to put His finger on. I feel responsible for their safety, often praying for their protection. I pray for them to be united with others in the faith. _____%.

2. <u>I recruit them</u>. I want to be able to inform and assure people that God has a call on their lives. I want to be one of those who bring people into specific paths which will produce discipleship in them. _____%.

3. <u>I hang out with them</u>. I tend to be quite friendly and people find me easy to talk to. I like to learn about them and enjoy just being in their presence. I want to help them learn to relate more effectively. I'm especially interested in forging strong friendships. _____%.

4. <u>I teach them</u>. I like to help people see the big picture and get hold of what is really real. I like to live out and relay principles to others. I enjoy helping people understand what life is all about. _____%.

5. <u>I apprentice them</u>. I have acquired some practical skills in getting things done and would like to share those skills with others in a hands-on, side-by-side partnership with them. It would please me to see others acquire these skills. _____%

6. <u>I debrief them</u>. God has given me an ability to observe people and realize the kinds of things they need to mature in character and ability. I manage to share these things with them in a way they can accept and profit from. _____%

7. <u>I get them anointed</u>. God seems to be able to use me to tell people about the power of the Holy Spirit and to pray for them so that they, too, become empowered by the Spirit. _____%

8. <u>Who is God leading me to</u>? As I think about the people in my congregation or fellowship group or organization, who does my attention keep returning to? Who does God seem to have ready for one or more of these seven things done for him or her?

_____

_____

_____9. How will I go about offering discipleship to this person?

_____

_____

_____

_____

10. For how long should we agree to experiment with this discipleship relationship? _____ months.

11. Let's set a date when we will evaluate how the relationship is going and whether we want to extend it for another time period or conclude it?

_____.

12. I will begin to take action on this by _____ date.

---

[1] Those who want to explore vulnerability in depth may want to read my book Holy Vulnerability.
[2] I'm indebted to C. Peter Wagner for this realization.

Mike Flynn is Director of FreshWind Ministries, which conducts conferences and seminars in Power Ministry, Healing, Leadership Development, and Spiritual Growth for churches, schools, and missions agencies. Mike has been an Episcopal priest since 1967.

He is also an Associate Vineyard Pastor. Biblically-based, experientially-tested ministries are taught, modeled, and imparted to participants in these events.

To explore the possibility of an event, please contact us at

FreshWind Ministries
4406 El Corazon Ct.
Camarillo, CA 93012
Phone and Fax: 805-383-1269
Email: mkfln@aol.com

To see more detailed information about the ministry, log onto *www.freshwindministries.org*

Mike has written several other books which are fully detailed on the website:

Holy Vulnerability, 1990
Inner Healing, 1993
The Mustard Seed Book, 1997
How To Be Good Without Really Trying, 2004

These books can be ordered from Mike or amazon.com.

FreshWind
MINISTRIES